REINALDO DOMINGOS

Journal of Dreams

ILLUSTRATIONS
BRUNA ASSIS BRASIL

THIS BOOK FEATURES INTERACTIVE CONTENT WITH AUGMENTED REALITY TECHNOLOGY.
TO EXPERIENCE THE UNIVERSE OF NICO AND HIS FRIENDS MORE CLOSELY, DOWNLOAD JOURNAL OF DREAMS APP (SEE QR CODE IN PAGE 5). INTERACTIVE PAGES ARE IDENTIFIED WITH THIS ICON.

PRESIDENT | REINALDO DOMINGOS
PEDAGOGICAL DIRETOR | ANA ROSA O. VILCHES SOPRANI
EDITORIAL COORDINATOR | CHRISTINE BAPTISTA AND RENATA DE SÁ
ILLUSTRATIONS | BRUNA ASSIS BRASIL
SCRIPT | DANIELA NASCIMENTO
TRANSLATION | ANDRE PASOTTO, GINA ADELE GATO E SHALIMAR FODRA
TECHNOLOGY | RBW COMUNICAÇÃO E STUDIO ZYX

1st edition in English, 2018

Av. Paulista, 726 – Cj. 1210 – Bela Vista
CEP: 01310-910 – São Paulo – SP
Tel.: 11 3177-7800
www.editoradsop.com.br

INTERNATIONAL CATALOGING DATA IN THE PUBLICATION (CIP)
(CÂMARA BRASILEIRA DO LIVRO, SP, BRASIL)

Domingos, Reinaldo
Journal of Dreams / Reinaldo Domingos;
Ilustrations Bruna Assis Brasil. -- 1. ed. --
São Paulo : Editora DSOP, 2018

ISBN 978-85-8276-327-8

1 Money - Children and juvenile Literature
2 Finances - Children and juvenile Literature
I. Brazil, Bruna Assis. II Title

18-22473 CDD-028.5

SYSTEMATIC CATALOG INDEXES
1- Financial Literacy : Children and juvenile Literature
2 Financial Education : Children and juvenile Literature 028.5

MY DEAR READERS,

Through *Journal of Dreams*, I am lucky enough to talk, all at the same time, to children, young people, and adults (who, by the way, are still children for a lifetime, are they not?).

As a financial educator and therapist, I am delighted to know that together we are contributing to a new generation of children and families with sound financial competence, who understand how to reach their lifegoals. The innovative concept in this book will help children, young people, and adults to use their money in a harmonious and balanced way, and to realize that money is just a means for achieving goals, not an end in itself. The **DSOP Methodology** uses a behavioral approach based on human science, not only mathematics, to introduce financial education as a tool for making dreams come true.

As a messenger for financial education in Brazil and in the world, I hope that together we can be part of new financial awareness for the future generations. I wish you happy reading and happy learning!

My warmest thanks!

REINALDO DOMINGOS

HI, I AM NICO.
HI, I AM MARIA, NICO'S MOTHER
HI, I AM AMADEU, NICO'S GRANDFATHER
HI, I AM PAULO, NICO'S FATHER
HI, I AM LELÊ, NICO'S SISTER

ABOUT THE EXPERIENCE WITH INTERACTIVITY

After reading Journal of Dreams, show the child the icon on pages 11, 13, 15, 20 and 27, go back to the pages to show it to the child. The interactive experience proposed by the book is the Augmented Reality (RA), briefly explain that it is a technology that blends the real and the virtual world, in this case, opening a new possibility for interacting even more with the characters in the book, since the illustrations will become "alive". Must use an electronic device (smartphone or tablet), the device will show the objects on the pages, but now in motion. On pages 11, 13, 15, 20 and 27, the activities contain voice and sound effects so that the child can assimilate the message proposed by the book in a much fun way.

How it works?

1. Download the "*Diário dos Sonhos*" app at Apple Store or Google Play or you can use the **QR Code** next to this text or in the Parents' Supplement, scan it and download the app.

2. After downloading and installing the app, open it and follow the steps that will be indicated on the screen so that you can see the Augmented Reality.

3. Place your smartphone or tablet on the page of the book that has the interactivity icon, view the Augmented Reality on the screen of your device, sometimes you need to scan the page so the device can capture the "signal" and show the images.

CONSTRUCTION

Le Monde
Le Monde
Modern Screen

SHORT-TERM DREAM ____________________

Draw your currency coins and add the values in the spaces below.

SUBTOTAL

______

______

______

______

______

______

TOTAL ____________________

Draw your currency paper money and add the values in the spaces below.

SUBTOTAL ____________

SUBTOTAL ____________

____

____

____

____

TOTAL ____________

MEDIUM-TERM DREAM

Draw your currency coins and add the values in the spaces below.

SUBTOTAL

TOTAL

Draw your currency paper money and add the values in the spaces below.

SUBTOTAL

SUBTOTAL

TOTAL

LONG-TERM DREAM

Draw your currency coins and add the values in the spaces below.

SUBTOTAL

TOTAL

Draw your currency paper money and add the values in the spaces below.

SUBTOTAL

SUBTOTAL

TOTAL

REINALDO DOMINGOS

Reinaldo Domingos is a teacher, educator, financial therapist and Post doctoral student at Florida Christian University, with a thesis on the **DSOP Methodology**. Author of the bestselling *Financial Therapy* and several books aimed at adult, juvenile and children's readership, he has written the series *The Boy and the Money* and *The Boy of Money*; and the books *The Boy of Money in Cordel*; *Having Money is no Secret*; *The ABCD of Financial Education* and *Children's Allowance is not just Money*. He is also the author of two series of textbooks on Financial Literacy for Brazilian primary education, adopted by a number of public and private schools. With a BSc in Accounting, postgraduate degree in Systems Analysis, and MSc in Business Administration from Florida Christian University, Reinaldo founded Confirp Consultant Accounting. He is currently president of the DSOP Group. He is creator, founder and president of Abefin – the Brazilian Association of Financial Educators. He is also the director of the first post-graduate course in Financial Education (face-to-face and online learning) in Brazil. Reinaldo is the mentor of the **DSOP Methodology**, which is the foundation of all the DSOP Financial Education Programs.